THE LAST HEATH HEN

Hardback ISBN: 978-0-9985725-6-7

Paperback ISBN: 978-0-9985725-7-4

Interior and Cover Art: Michael Berndt
Formatting: Rose M. Kern

Published through RMK Publications, LLC

Maps provided by Michael Berndt and Martha's Vineyard Museum
Photo of plaque: Rob Lowrance
Photo of Heath Hens gathered: New York Museum of Natural History exhibit, provided by Bill Hubick, Maryland Biodiversity Project

The printing of this edition was made possible by the Cape Cod Museum of Natural History in Brewster and its affiliate, The Thornton W. Burgess Society in Sandwich, Massachusetts, whose missions are to inspire appreciation, understanding and stewardship of our natural environment and wildlife through discovery and learning.

THE LAST HEATH HEN

By

Christie Palmer Lowrance

Illustrated by Michael Berndt

To Bill

Who shares love of fair winds and clear skies

with all creatures of the air

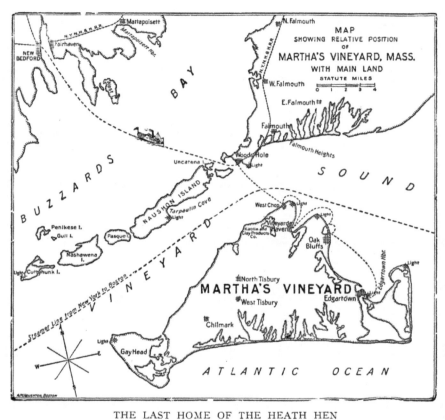

THE LAST HOME OF THE HEATH HEN
The great plain lies in the triangle formed by West Tisbury, Edgartown and
Vineyard Haven.

The island of Martha's Vineyard

Reprinted from 1934 pamphlet "The Heath Hen's Journey to
Extinction" by Henry Beetle Hough

Many years ago, something extraordinary happened on Martha's Vineyard, something that had never happened before and would never happen again.

It was a rainy spring morning in 1931 on the big island that lies just south of Falmouth, Massachusetts on Cape Cod, a pretty sight across the few miles of saltwater that separate them. On a clear day, you could see the white wake of ferry boats churning across Vineyard Sound between the island and the mainland.

But not that day.

A Cape Cod ferry approaching Martha's Vineyard

The air was weighted and wet, and a raw wind blew across the open field where two men, a biologist and a writer, crouched inside an observation box with peepholes in the sides, hiding and waiting. The bad weather was terrible for their purpose. They almost cancelled their plans, but time was running out. They had few options.

Suddenly, the object of their quest emerged from low trees and scrub brush at the edge of the field, soggy and bedraggled, almost unrecognizable. "There he is!" one man whispered softly to his companion.

It was Booming Ben.

A wild bird walked slowly onto the field, cautious and wary. Chicken-sized with a short tail, he had lovely brown-and-white barred feathers that gave him perfect protective coloring. When he froze motionless on the ground, it was almost impossible to see him, even if you knew exactly where he was. The bird pecked in the low grass, casually going about the business of searching for food.

Eventually he came upon the box-shaped blind. Without hesitation he began eating yellow cracked corn that had been hand-scattered on the ground nearby. Oblivious to any danger, Booming Ben walked right into a trap.

Thornton Burgess and Alfred Gross peering out of
the observation blind.

Although the small, wooden hut concealed the two men, they barely breathed for fear of alarming keen eyes and sharp ears. Inside one man tightly held a string attached to the stick that propped open the trap. If he pulled it, a large, domed mesh cover would drop down, holding captive any bird or animal underneath. It was now or never. He looked questioningly at his partner who nodded silently. With one swift jerk, the trap fell.

Dr. Alfred Gross and Thornton Burgess, a biology professor and a children's author, had captured the world's last Heath Hen!

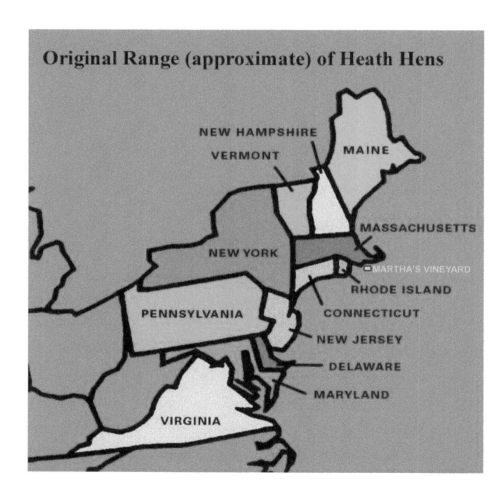

Original Range (approximate) of Heath Hens

NEW HAMPSHIRE

VERMONT

MAINE

MASSACHUSETTS

NEW YORK

MARTHA'S VINEYARD

RHODE ISLAND

CONNECTICUT

PENNSYLVANIA

NEW JERSEY

DELAWARE

MARYLAND

VIRGINIA

12

Once these game birds thrived from Maine and New Hampshire to Virginia. Some people think Pilgrims and Native Americans may have eaten Heath Hens at their thanksgiving feast. The birds were related to Prairie Chickens, members of the large Grouse family that still lives in many parts of the United States.

But eventually, due to hunting and land development, Heath Hens found the environment they needed to survive in only one place: the island of Martha's Vineyard.

Every creature, wild or tame, must have certain conditions to satisfy its particular needs for food, water, and safe shelter. The habitat that Heath Hens preferred was not shady woods or open grassy meadows, but low, scrubby brush that gave them ground protection and plenty of berries, seeds, insects and plants to eat.

blueberries

Favorite Foods
of the
Heath Hen

bayberries

partridge
berries

ants &
worms

seeds & acorns

grass & clover

Scientists, conservationists, and islanders became worried about the Heath Hen. What would happen if this bird's numbers continued to shrink smaller and smaller?

In 1908 they decided to set aside a little more than 600 acres for a Heath Hen reservation. Known as a sandplain, this large, flat, dry, sandy expanse was an ideal habitat for the birds. More land was added later, and today the reserve is part of the 5,000-acre Manuel Correllus State Forest.

They even appointed a special guardian of this land to help provide food and protection from poachers and predators like cats and hawks.

The 1916 fire on Martha's Vineyard

It was a good plan. A little more than five years later there were nearly 2,000 Heath Hens on the Vineyard, and people believed the birds had been saved. But then, in 1916, a great fire broke out. It burned nearly 13,000 acres, about twenty percent of the island, including much of the Heath Hen reservation.

Whipped by strong winds, flames spread rapidly, just at the time when female birds were sitting on their nests. Apparently, many refused to flee and died with their chicks and eggs. After the fire, not only were there fewer Heath Hens, but now there were far fewer female than male birds.

That same winter a large influx of hungry goshawks from northern woods arrived on the island. With so much ground cover destroyed, these powerful hunters found Heath Hens easy to catch, and, worse, winter the next year was especially harsh. In just a year, the Heath Hen population plummeted to less than 150 birds.

Goshawk attacking a Heath Hen

Scientists, conservationists, and the people of Martha's Vineyard became more worried than ever. What could be done?

They needed an expert. State officials hired bird specialist Dr. Alfred Gross, an ornithologist at Bowdoin College in Brunswick, Maine who knew a great deal about the Grouse family. They asked him to come study the situation on Martha's Vineyard and make a yearly count, or census, of the number of Heath Hens he and others saw.

Hopefully, his research would help people understand what was happening to birds that once lived throughout so much of the East Coast. He invited his good friend Thornton Burgess, a respected naturalist and children's author, to join him.

How is it *possible* to count individual birds on a large island?

One thing made it easy. Every spring during mating season, male and female Heath Hens on Martha's Vineyard gathered together. If there were many birds, they chose a few favorite meeting spots, called *leks*, but when there were fewer birds, they gathered in only one place.

Fluffing out their feathers, the male Heath Hens dropped their wings to the ground like turkeys, spread out their short tail feathers like fans, and lifted long feathers on both sides of their necks straight up, like rabbit ears.

Photo of New York Museum of Natural History exhibit

They strutted proudly about, sometimes rushing at a rival or stamping their feet as if the earth itself was their personal drum. Suddenly, excited birds would leap three or four feet into the air, twisting around like a corkscrew before they landed.

What a bizarre sight these birds made as they danced and pranced and stamped and twirled, all to gain the admiring attention of female Heath Hens who sat quietly nearby, pretending not to notice them at all.

Strangest of all, the males inflated bright orange sacs the size of tennis balls on the sides of their necks.

With these sacs they could make a peculiar booming sound, so loud it could be heard a mile away. But people couldn't tell what direction the sound came from, or even how to describe it! Was it like a distant tugboat tooting in the island fog? Or someone blowing across the top of an empty bottle or into a conch shell? Or witches groaning? Or monks chanting?

People did agree, however, that a field of male Heath Hens cackling and hooting and tooting and stamping and booming sounded like *nothing* anybody had ever heard or seen before. The several places Heath Hens gathered for their strange courtship performances on Martha's Vineyard were known as booming grounds.

But for many complicated reasons – from disease, fire, and stray cats to illegal poaching and too few females – the birds' population continued to decline. When Thornton Burgess joined Dr. Gross for the 1928 Heath Hen census, they found just three birds, all males.

This was dreadful news. Without females, the species could not produce a new generation of Heath Hen chicks.

In 1929, only one bird appeared on the booming ground near Jimmy Green's farm in West Tisbury. He looked plump and healthy.

But to Thornton Burgess and Alfred Gross, who were conducting the survey from their blind, the lone bird was a heart-breaking sight as he appeared out of the scrub brush, alert, listening and looking intently for another Heath Hen.

"The display, dance and call were repeated many times, the bird occasionally stopping to pick up a few grains of corn," Thornton Burgess remembered. "It was sheer stark tragedy… I knew that nowhere in all the world was there a mate or even a companion for him."

The people of Martha's Vineyard affectionately named the last Heath Hen Booming Ben.

When Thornton Burgess and Alfred Gross climbed into their cramped hut on that cold, rainy spring day, hoping to trap Booming Ben, they knew they couldn't save him or the species. But they could possibly help others learn the fate of the last Heath Hen.

They would capture him and put numbered identification bands on both legs. If he was ever found, people would know this was Booming Ben, not, somehow, another one of his kind. And they would document him and the event with photographs and videos.

So, they set the trap and waited anxiously in the
blind.

As soon as the large mesh cover fell, Dr. Gross rushed out of the blind, slipping twice in his desperate effort to grab the startled bird before it broke a wing trying to escape.

Then he handed Booming Ben carefully to Thornton Burgess who held the bird gently while the ornithologist fastened on two bands: an aluminum band, engraved with "407880" on his left leg and a copper one engraved with "A-634024" on his right.

Thornton Burgess holding Booming Ben

They had managed to catch and band Booming Ben. So, what would they do next?

They knew they could give him to a zoo to live out his days in captivity, like the last passenger pigeon.

Or they could release him back into nature, to spend the rest of his life – whether days or years – free and wild.

They decided to set Booming Ben free.

Dr. Gross held Booming Ben for just a moment and lightly smoothed his beautiful, soft feathers, a small, respectful farewell. When he set the wild bird back on the ground and opened his hands, he knew no one might ever see him again.

Booming Ben immediately disappeared into the safety of nearby bushes. To the delight of the scientist and the writer, he returned the next day as if nothing unusual had happened.

Except for a few sightings the following year, however, Booming Ben never re-appeared on the booming ground. No one knows for certain what happened to him because the numbered legs bands have never been found, and the reward for returning them has never been claimed.

(One family of summer visitors believed their car had hit and killed the famous bird, but they were too ashamed to tell anyone, and swore each other to secrecy.)

In 1933 Dr. Gross officially declared the Heath Hen, known formally to scientists as *Tympanuchus cupido cupido*, to be extinct.

Environmental officials say that it was the only instance of the last member of species in the United States being documented in the wild.

The decades-long effort to save Heath Hens from extinction on Martha's Vineyard was also one of the first species conservation program in the world.

Why did scientists and conservationists and the people of Martha's Vineyard try so hard to save this beautiful wild bird that danced and pranced, stamped and twirled, boomed and hooted and tooted?

Why was Booming Ben, the last Heath Hen, so important to people?

For the same reason that you and I are important.

In all the world,

  there was only one race of Heath Hens.

In all the world,

  there was only one Booming Ben.

In all the world,

  there is only one you and only one me.

And when there is only one of something, it is very important to take good care of it.

THE END

MORE INFORMATION ...

Complex questions and fascinating issues arise out of the story and history of the last Heath Hens!

Here are a few topics to think about:

HOW DID HEATH HENS GET TO MARTHA'S VINEYARD?

No one knows for sure, of course, but it is most likely that centuries ago a flock flew across Vineyard Sound from the mainland or one of the nearby Elizabeth Islands.

WHAT IS THE DIFFERENCE BETWEEN A SPECIES AND A SUBSPECIES?

To a scientist, a lot! They must be very careful about their descriptions of all living and non-living things, from rocks and trees to mongooses and bacteria and Heath Hens. Even the smallest similarities and differences help scientists understand ancient and current growth and development of all life forms, and how they interact, thrive and survive.

The Heath Hen was part of a large family of birds, the Grouse family. This family includes the Greater and Lesser Prairie Chicken, the Ruffed Grouse, the Red Grouse, and others, as well as the Heath Hen. Its closest relative is the Prairie Chicken; in fact, some people considered the Heath Hen the Eastern Prairie Chicken.

WHO WERE THORNTON BURGESS AND DR. ALFRED GROSS?

Dr. Alfred Gross was an ornithologist, an academic expert on birds. He taught biology at Bowdoin College in Brunswick, Maine. In the early 1920s, he was studying parasites that infected the Ruffed Grouse in New England. When Thornton Burgess learned that the scientist needed more bird specimens to study, he enthusiastically offered to help.

At that time, Thornton Burgess was a popular naturalist and the author of dozens of children's books. Radio technology had just been developed commercially. People in their homes would gather eagerly around a radio set to listen to the few programs available. In 1924 Burgess introduced listeners to a special nature program for children called the Radio Nature League. Within weeks, he had thousands of listeners, some as far away as England!

Thornton Burgess believed that radios could be useful to science because they could reach so many people at once. He told his listeners to send specimens of Ruffed Gross to Dr. Gross to study. (It was then hunting season and Ruffed Grouse were popular game birds.) That fall the scientist was amazed when he received 300 birds to examine, far more than the 40 or 50 he expected.

He and Thornton Burgess were both interested in birds, photography, nature, and conservation, and became lifelong best friends. Their still and moving films of the Heath Hens on Martha's Vineyard have become an important record of an extinct species.

FIRE AND WILDLIFE

People often think wildfires in nature are bad for wildlife and the environment, but the opposite can be true. Wildfires can be helpful by destroying certain types of plants that crowd out native species. The ashes that remain can also help the growth of new, young plants that provide good food for animals.

CATS

In 1913, Dr. William Hornaday, a conservation activist and director of the organization that was later the Bronx Zoo, wrote a book, *Our Vanishing Wildlife*. He listed species of birds that had become or were nearing extinction in the 48 states in America more than 100 years ago. It also listed the causes of extinctions. Among those causes were cats, domestic and feral (domestic cats living in the wild). In this story, cats were known to contribute to the demise of the Heath Hen. Today, leading conservation organizations estimate that cats kill 2.4 billion birds a year nationwide.

JIMMY GREEN

Jimmy Green was a native of Barbados in the Caribbean and a former whaler and ferryboat fireman. Perhaps he came to the Vineyard as a mariner and decided to become a farmer? His West Tisbury farm was important to the Heath Hens because it became the last place where they and Booming Ben lived. He was glad to help Alfred Gross and others use his fields to observe, study, and keep track of the last Heath Hens. Nearby is a plaque in honor of these birds.

HEATH HEN
TYMPANUCHUS CUPIDO CUPIDO

THE SOLE REMAINING HEATH HEN IN THE WORLD WAS SEEN FOR THE LAST TIME NEAR THIS SPOT ON MARCH 11, 1932; THIS EASTERN RACE OF THE GREATER PRAIRIE CHICKEN WAS DECLARED EXTINCT IN 1933. DURING MATING SEASON, THE MALES MADE A LOUD "BOOMING" SOUND BY INFLATING THE ORANGE AIR SACS ON THEIR NECKS, A SOUND THAT COULD BE HEARD AS FAR AS ONE MILE AWAY. A STAPLE IN THE EARLY COLONISTS' DIET, THE HEATH HEN WAS MORE IMPORTANT THAN THE WILD TURKEY TO THE SURVIVAL OF THE PILGRIMS AT PLYMOUTH COLONY IN THE HARD WINTER OF 1620-1621. DESPITE THE PASSAGE OF VARIOUS PROTECTIVE LAWS, BY 1845 THE ONLY BIRDS LEFT WERE ON MARTHA'S VINEYARD, HAVING ONCE BEEN WIDESPREAD FROM COASTAL NEW ENGLAND SOUTH AT LEAST TO MARYLAND. IN 1908 THE COMMONWEALTH OF MASSACHUSETTS SET ASIDE 600 ACRES HERE AS A HEATH HEN RESERVATION. ADDITIONAL LAND WAS ADDED LATER UNTIL THE RESERVATION TOTALED NEARLY 5,000 ACRES, MOST OF WHICH ULTIMATELY BECAME THE MANUEL F. CORRELLUS STATE FOREST. THE HEATH HEN THRIVED ON THE RESERVATION, ITS NUMBERS RISING FROM ABOUT 50 IN 1908 TO ABOUT 2,000 IN EARLY 1916. BUT IN MAY 1916 A GREAT FIRE SWEPT THE RESERVATION, DESTROYING MANY NESTING FEMALES AND THEIR EGGS, REDUCING THE POPULATION TO ABOUT 150. PRIMARILY DUE TO INBREEDING, DISEASE AND PREDATION, DESPITE EFFORTS TO PROTECT AND PROPAGATE THE BIRD, ITS NUMBERS SLOWLY DWINDLED TO 28 IN 1923, ABOUT 50 IN 1927, AND ONLY 3 IN 1928; THE LAST BIRD, KNOWN AS "BOOMING BEN", LIVED ALONE FROM 1929 UNTIL 1932.

BANDING

In this story, bird banding plays a unique and important role. The following additional information has been provided by Wayne Petersen, Mass Audubon field ornithologist.

WHAT DOES IT MEAN TO "BAND" A BIRD?

To band a bird is to put a unique numbered ring on a bird's leg so that if it's ever recaptured or found dead somewhere, the information on the band can be returned to the Bird Banding Office (bandreports@usgs.gov) so that both the original bander and the finder of the band can be notified that the band and the bird have been recovered along with where and when it was found, the species of bird if possible, and which leg the band was on. The band will have information on it to let the finder know how to report it.

IS IT HARD TO BAND A BIRD?

It's not too difficult once you know how to do it, but it requires a license that indicates someone is certified to do it. Often the most difficult part of bird banding is capturing birds, especially if they are small birds and need to be removed from mist nets set in wooded areas. This takes a lot of practice and a degree of manual dexterity to avoid hurting the bird as it's removed from a net. For larger birds like waterfowl, raptors, Heath Hens (!), etc., the trapping procedure is different but the process is similar once the bird is captured.

DOES IT HURT THE BIRD?

Done properly by an experienced bander, it should not hurt the bird at all, and once a bird is banded, it's like a person wearing a ring on their finger.

DO PEOPLE BAND BIG BIRDS LIKE CROWS AND HAWKS AND TINY BIRDS LIKE HUMMINGBIRDS?

Yes, but as noted above, the techniques for capturing the birds is different, and for tiny birds like hummers, or really large birds like cranes, the bands and the banding techniques are obviously quite different.

DO BANDS STAY ON FOREVER? CAN A BIRD GET TANGLED IN BRUSH OR LIMBS BECAUSE IT HAS A BAND ON?

Some bands last pretty much forever, but for long-lived birds, or seabirds that are constantly in saltwater, sometimes a band will need to be replaced if the bird is recaptured with a worn band. It's very rare for a band to become entangled in vegetation. Again, it's similar to a ring on your finger that won't bother the bird.

WHO KEEPS THE RECORDS OF THE BIRD BANDINGS?

The bander has to keep records, and he/she must annually send it the banding data from each season. The data that's submitted is then kept in a giant, computerized database at the U.S. Bird Banding Office so if a band is recovered, it can be tracked back to the bander with all the attendant data.

HOW ARE THE RECORDS USEFUL?

The records are very useful and contribute all kinds of information about longevity, migratory destinations, changes in plumage, distribution, etc. This is the real reason that bird-banding is done, and has been done for so many years.

ABOUT THE BOOK

Christie Palmer Lowrance

As the author of a definitive biography on 20th century naturalist and children's author, Thornton W. Burgess, I was moved to tears in reading his account of watching the last Heath Hen on Martha's Vineyard, Booming Ben as the Vineyarders named him, emerge alone from scrub brush onto his species' mating grounds in the final years of the 1920s. This was the sole bird of its kind, without a mate or even a companion to answer his questioning calls.

Burgess was a master storyteller, but the story of the last Heath Hen needed no imaginative touches because Burgess was an eye-witness to the tragic scene. In researching the survey work conducted by biologist Dr. Alfred Gross of Bowdoin College and his invitation to Burgess to join him on the Vineyard, I was powerfully struck by the realization that once the last Heath Hen, a male, was captured, his fate was entirely in the hands of those two men who banded and briefly held the bird: They could have the body preserved by taxidermy for future generations to see. They could send him to a zoo to live out his remaining days in captivity. Or they could release him.

That they chose the bird's freedom will be a relief to readers as it was to me, but that this was Gross and Burgess' decision alone to make was astonishing. I consulted Mark Madison, senior historian of U.S. Fisheries and Wildlife, was this possible? Yes, he said, in that day, it was.

Children are familiar with the threat of extinction, from movies of fearsome dinosaurs to TV ads seeking financial support for endangered tigers. But *The Last Heath Hen* is a true story about a species of bird that vanished relatively recently on the Massachusetts island of Martha's Vineyard.

This book documents the lengthy and concerted effort to save the Heath Hen made by organizations, institutions, and individuals responsible for conservation. Why did they fail?

Let children digest and understand how complicated conservation is: even on this small scale, with a small bird on a small island, the best efforts failed.

"Children learn soon enough the hardship of life," author Thornton Burgess told critics who chastised him for consistently writing stories in which predators like Reddy Fox *never* caught prey like Peter Rabbit.

When I was pondering how I could possibly bring this subject of unmitigated loss to a child without causing despair, the book's final message came to me: we make the effort because life, *all life*, in its grand and glorious diversity matters. It will *always* matter.

Two rich resources for my Heath Hen research were the Brunswick College Library Archives and *Hope Is A Thing With Feathers* by Christopher Cokinos. My thanks to them both, as well as appreciation for the information provided by Mass Audubon ornithologist, Wayne Petersen, and Vineyard authorities, Tom Chase, Linsey Lee, and research librarian, Bow Van Riper.

www.christielowrance.com

ABOUT THE ILLUSTRATIONS

Michael Berndt

I'm a longtime artist, experienced in acrylic paint, mostly landscape and portraiture. However, I have never illustrated a book before, children's or adult, so this project posed some unique challenges for me. I was asked to create a series of illustrations depicting the efforts to save the Heath Hen, efforts that ultimately did not succeed, as this book details.

I needed to make sure the images that were illustrating Christie's writing all worked together cohesively as one body of work. I also needed to ensure the content achieved a high level of accuracy due to the historical significance and biological nature of the subject matter.

At the start of the project, I had no knowledge of the story of the Heath Hen, no idea what a Heath Hen even looked like, or who Thornton Burgess and Alfred Gross were. So I began with research, then sketches and ideas that Christie and I discussed.

These collaborative sessions with Christie were the foundation of what would develop into the finished images. Because of her depth of knowledge and expertise on the subject matter, she had a clear vision of what she wanted these images to represent, and she was an excellent resource when it came to getting the details right. But she was also open-minded and willing to defer to me when it came to the more artistic issues like composition and color palette.

From these discussions I developed an overall tone and style which I applied to each individual image. Of course, there were variations as well - the image of the Heath Hen standing proud in the sunrise has a brighter, more vibrant tone, while the painting of the devastating fire is dark and foreboding. This latter work was perhaps the most technically challenging to me, and I avoided it until nearly the end of the project.

What became one of my most important resources was an old 1930s film. Thanks to the online archive at Bowdoin College in Brunswick, Maine, where Alfred Gross had been a biology professor, I was able to see a masterfully restored film created by Dr. Gross that chronicled the fateful day he and Burgess captured, banded and released dear Booming Ben, the subject of this work. This film not only provided me with many important visual references, it also connected me with the subject in a deeply emotional way. This connection is what prompted me to begin this project by painting Thornton Burgess holding the Heath Hen, an image which, for me, holds massive emotional weight.

I'd like to offer my thanks to Bowdoin College for providing this resource and I recommend that anyone interested in further understanding this story watch the film. It is beautiful and absolutely heart wrenching.

RESOURCES

American Bird Conservancy (www. abcbirds.org)

Audubon Society (www.audubonva.org)

Bird Banding Laboratory | U.S. Geological Survey (usgs.gov)

Bowdoin College Library Special Collections and Archives (library@bowdoin.edu)

Cape Cod Museum of Natural History (www.ccmnh.org)

Martha's Vineyard Museum (www.mvmuseum.org)

Maryland Biodiversity Project (www.marylandbiodiversity.com)

Nature's Ambassador: The Legacy of Thornton W. Burgess (www.christielowrance.com)

Thornton W. Burgess Society (www.thorntonburgess.org)

Cape Cod Museum of Natural History

869 Main Street/Route 6A
Brewster, MA 02631
508.896.3867
http://www.ccmnh.org

Thornton W. Burgess Society & Green Briar Nature Center & Jam Kitchen

6 Discovery Hill Road
East Sandwich, MA 02537
508.888.6870
http://www.thorntonburgess.org

The printing of this edition was made possible by the Cape Cod Museum of Natural History in Brewster, and its affiliate, The Thornton W. Burgess Society in Sandwich, Massachusetts, whose missions are to inspire appreciation, understanding and stewardship of our natural environment and wildlife through discovery and learning.

What do you see in Nature?

The next few pages are for making notes or drawing pictures of the wildlife and natural environment around you.

Wildlife Observations & Drawings

Wildlife Observations & Drawings

Wildlife Observations & Drawings

Wildlife Observations & Drawings

Wildlife Observations & Drawings

Wildlife Observations & Drawings

Wildlife Observations & Drawings

Wildlife Observations & Drawings